Made with 100% recycled FSC certified paper.

FSC

A000523

FOR MORE SUPPORT WITH YOUR DREAMS SCAN HERE

THESE DREAMS BELONG TO:

_____

The top regret people have at the end of their life is not regretting something they did, it's regretting something they didn't do.

PURPOSE OF THIS JOURNAL

This journal is a safe place for your dreams to live. It is a place where you can track and update your dreams as you, and they, evolve over time. This journal is designed to help you overcome the greatest barriers that will stop you from achieving your goals. The following pages will help you take tangible steps toward your goals and help you achieve them.

Our personal goals often take the back burner in our busy lives. They are the first things to fall through the cracks of our packed schedules, and most of us push our personal goals until it's too late. When we reach our final days we regret the things we didn't do, not the things we did.

When researchers from Cornell University asked thousands of people on their deathbed to name the biggest regret in their entire life, 76% of participants had the same answer: "Not fulfilling my ideal self."[1]

This statistic broke my heart, and it became a turning point in my life. My mission became not only to ensure that I didn't end up in that 76%, but also to help as many people as I could to not end up there either. It's wild to think that over three-quarters of the population will reach the end of their life and think, "Damn. I wish I'd had the courage to live a life true to myself, not the life that others expected of me."

The goal of *The Bucket List Journal* is simple: ensure that you do not reach your deathbed regretting the things you did not do.

My bucket list transformed my life. It changed the realities of my friends and my family, and I believe it has the power to change your life, too.

Ben.

A LIST CHANGED MY LIFE

In college, I was oblivious to the power of a bucket list. It was my freshman year, and I was preoccupied with the "shoulds" - consumed by the pressure to succeed academically and athletically. While training for what I thought was my biggest dream, playing in the Rugby World Cup with the Under-19 Canadian national team, I began feeling anxiety about making my field goals. Worry crept into my mind at night. "What if I miss an easy kick directly in front of the goal posts at the World Cup?" Losing sleep became normal for me. Before I knew it, my anxiety was crippling. I had slid into a debilitating depression.

This was nothing I'd ever experienced before. I'd always been a happy-go-lucky guy with a supportive group of family and friends. But now, I was at the point where I found it too daunting to get myself to school and rugby practice—and before I knew it, I was dropped from both the university and the national rugby team.

In hindsight, I'm not even quite sure how this happened, but I became a complete shut-in. I was unable to leave my parents' house. In the dead of night, I felt so deeply terrified of the emptiness getting worse that I would keep a night-light on. I was essentially a full grown man afraid of the dark. I felt like I was slowly suffocating. The pillars of my life were collapsing around me yet I just continued to sit there frozen. I was trapped under a pile of "shoulds", unable to move. I was, in a word, buried.

I did what a lot of people do. I tried to push through and I avoided professional help. I endured these feelings for months before a few friends insisted that I join them to live and work for the summer in a small ski town a few hours away. Slowly, I began to emerge from my fog. I landed a job and started gaining some self-confidence. I started talking about how I was really feeling to my friends and ultimately a therapist. And I met other people my age who inspired me—one who was starting his own business, others who were traveling the world. I realized that I felt energized around these people and I wanted more of that feeling. As the summer wound down, I made a decision. I was determined to only surround myself with people who inspired me.

Little did I know then, this one small decision would completely change my life.

While pursuing relationships with inspiring people, I found three friends—Jonnie, Duncan, and Dave—who were also grappling with the same sense of feeling buried. We reckoned the quickest way to unbury our true selves was to ask the question, "What do you want to do before you die?"

Confronting our mortality quickly snapped our lives into perspective. Our collective answers resulted in what looked like the world's most insane bucket list: 100 things we wanted to do before we die.

Some of the items on the list were simple (#14: Grow a Mustache or #34: Pay for Someone's Groceries), but most of them were down-right nuts (#100: Go to Space or #99: Host Saturday Night Live). Our list morphed into a mission: hit the open road and attempt to live out 100 of our wildest dreams. For each list item we accomplished we agreed to help a total stranger cross something off their bucket list.

It was a harebrained scheme, born of a potent mix of ambition, naivete, and raw fury over time already wasted deferring our dreams. Each of us had our own reasons for enlisting and our own demons to overcome.

Then, Matthew Arnold came along. In his 1854 poem, "The Buried Life"—required reading for English 201—there were a few lines that articulated what we could hardly describe to each other after months of planning:

But often, in the world's most crowded streets,
But often, in the din of strife,
There rises an unspeakable desire
After the knowledge of our buried life...
A thirst to spend our fire and restless force
In tracking out our true, original course;
A longing to inquire
Into the mystery of this heart which beats
So wild, so deep in us — to know
Whence our lives come and where they go.

That was it! We weren't tracking our true, original course. We had dreams but they were constantly buried by the day-to-day. Life always seemed to get in the way and our dreams would get pushed to the back burner. We agreed to borrow the poem title from the wise, old poet and carry out our plan.

Our "plan" was a mess. On the eve of the road trip, a mechanic told us that the RV we'd borrowed wouldn't make it home. I had fabricated a long family wedding in order to get enough time off of work, and we pretended to own a production company to raise money for a camera and gas for the RV.

What could go wrong?

But we weren't thinking about that. This was about our list. The only thing we knew for sure was that we had two weeks to cross off as many items we'd written down as possible and help people along the way. We hit the road in our rickety RV.

It wasn't long before our adventures caught people's attention and emails flooded in from across the continent. Strangers asked for help doing anything you can imagine: tattoo design training, flights in an F-18 fighter jet, reconciliation with sons or mothers, riding a horse through a drive-thru. Others wrote to offer help with our list, sending invitations for bull rides, hot air balloon trips, and toasts at strangers' weddings. It seemed like we weren't alone in our quest for meaning. In a world tired of nagging gloom, a test of blind optimism struck a chord.

The two-week road trip never ended. It began in 2006 and the adventures and life lessons continue to unfold, year after year, as I continue to uncover a growing sense of purpose. With 96 of the original 100 list items completed, this mission has evolved to become much bigger than the list itself. It has become a mantra for life. The list is my compass, leading me toward a life of adventure and fulfilment.

I have changed and grown over the years, and my list has changed with me. I have added hundreds of new list items reflecting my evolving ambitions and passions. And when I get buried by the day-to-day, my list reminds me that my dreams haven't gone anywhere.

BEN'S LIST

1. ~~Open the six o'clock news~~
2. ~~Lead a parade~~
3. ~~Do the NYE Countdown in Times Square~~
4. ~~Start a dance in a public place~~
5. ~~Ride down a mountain on a longboard~~
6. ~~Have a beer with Prince Harry~~
7. ~~Plant a tree~~
8. ~~Play ball with President Obama~~
9. ~~Give a university commencement address~~
10. ~~Make someone's dream come true~~
11. ~~Destroy a computer~~
12. ~~Swim with giant sea turtles~~
13. ~~Kiss the Stanley Cup~~
14. ~~Help someone build a house~~
15. ~~Grow a mustache~~
16. Make the cover of Rolling Stone
17. ~~Scuba dive the Great Barrier Reef~~
18. ~~Start a huge wave in a stadium~~
19. ~~Tell a joke on late-night television~~
20. ~~Write a #1 New York Times Bestselling book~~
21. ~~Get a song I've written on the radio~~
22. ~~Officiate a wedding~~
23. ~~Foster a dog~~
24. ~~Help my parents cross something off their list~~
25. ~~Go to a rock concert in all leather~~
26. ~~Solve a crime or capture a fugitive~~
27. Yell in court: You want the truth? You can't handle the truth!
28. ~~Give a stranger a $100 bill~~
29. ~~Send a message in a bottle~~
30. ~~Scream at the top of my lungs~~
31. ~~Make a big donation to charity~~
32. ~~Cut a ribbon at a major opening~~
33. ~~Get something named after you~~
34. ~~Compete in a krump competition~~
35. ~~Pay for someone's groceries~~
36. ~~Do a sketch with Will Ferrell~~
37. ~~Throw the first pitch at a Major League Baseball game~~
38. ~~Win and yell BINGO! at a bingo hall~~
39. ~~Climb inside the Egyptian pyramids~~
40. ~~Stand under a plane while it lands~~
41. ~~Make the front page of the newspaper~~
42. ~~Make a toast at a stranger's wedding~~
43. ~~Spend a night in jail~~
44. ~~Be a knight for a day~~
45. ~~Catch something and eat it~~
46. ~~Sleep in a haunted house~~
47. ~~Sing the national anthem before an NBA game~~
48. ~~Get in the Guinness Book of World Records~~
49. ~~Own a fainting goat~~
50. ~~Take a stranger out for dinner~~

51. ~~Streak a field~~

52. ~~Ride a camel in the desert~~

53. ~~Be a mentor~~

54. ~~Make a TV show~~

55. ~~Donate blood~~

56. ~~Be interviewed by Oprah~~

57. ~~Write an article for a major publication~~

58. ~~Learn how to meditate~~

59. ~~See a cadaver~~

60. ~~Ask out the girl of your dreams~~

61. ~~Go paragliding~~

62. ~~Paint a mural~~

63. ~~Join a protest for something that matters~~

64. ~~Build a successful business~~

65. ~~Visit Folsom Prison~~

66. ~~Learn how to sail~~

67. ~~Walk the red carpet~~

68. ~~Make wine~~

69. ~~Swim with sharks~~

70. ~~Snowball fight on a glacier~~

71. ~~Skydive over the Alps~~

72. ~~Take kids on a shopping spree~~

73. ~~Throw a legendary surprise party~~

74. ~~Make a music video~~

75. ~~Help deliver a stranger's baby~~

76. ~~Build a house in Joshua Tree, California~~

77. ~~Visit the Guinness factory in Dublin~~

78. ~~Go to Burning Man~~

79. ~~Fall in love~~

80. ~~Crash the MTV Video Music Awards~~

81. ~~Sail the Croatian Islands~~

82. ~~Meet The Lonely Island guys~~

83. ~~Make a hot chocolate hot tub~~

84. ~~Win an award~~

85. ~~Street perform and make $100~~

86. ~~Run a marathon~~

87. ~~Throw a party I remember on my deathbed~~

88. ~~Teach an elementary school class~~

89. ~~Live on a Kibbutz~~

90. ~~Escape from a deserted island~~

91. ~~Drive a Fiat across Italy~~

92. ~~Sleep in a Bedouin tent in the desert~~

93. ~~Mend a broken friendship~~

94. ~~Learn how to kite surf~~

95. ~~Race dune buggies~~

96. ~~Party with a rock star~~

97. ~~Host a lemonade stand~~

98. ~~Race horses~~

99. Host *Saturday Night Live*

100. Go to space

YOUR LIST IS IMPORTANT

Our most enduring regrets are the ones that stem from our failure to live up to our ideal selves. People are haunted more by regrets about failing to fulfill their hopes, goals, and aspirations than by regrets about failing to fulfill their duties, obligations, and responsibilities.

It's not enough to just "do the right thing." We need to establish that it's vital to act on our hopes and dreams, and that it's not normal to keep putting them off indefinitely. In the short term, we regret our actions more than inactions, but in the long term, the inaction regrets stick around longer.

Your list brings you closer to your ideal self: the person you won't regret being on your deathbed.

WHY WE PUT OFF OUR LIST

1.

We often assume we first need inspiration before we can strive to achieve our ideals. But research shows that's not true. Don't wait around for inspiration. That's just an excuse. We must create it through action. By taking steps toward our goal, we begin to feel inspired. As Rich Roll says, "Mood follows action." It's important to note that we don't need to know the path to success, we just need to know the first step. We can figure out the second step after the first. You are the architect of your own inspiration.

Problem: Waiting for inspiration
Solution: Create inspiration through action

2.

We are rarely pressed to think about deadlines for our personal goals. We have deadlines for every other task in our lives: work deadlines, rent payments, school assignments, car repairs. But we treat our personal goals as if they have no deadline, as if we'll always have tomorrow to make things happen. Most people continue to push these goals until they realize, sadly, that they are out of time.

How do we create deadlines for our bucket list? The answer is accountability. That's why the act of writing a list is key—it creates a small amount of accountability. Sharing your list is also powerful because you feel accountable to the people you share it with. If you want to increase your chances of success, find an accountability buddy. You're 77% more likely to achieve your goal if you have someone checking in on you down the line.

Problem: No deadlines
Solution: Create accountability

3.

Fear is the #1 thing holding us back from achieving our personal goals. It's either the fear of failure or the fear of what other people think about us.

The fear of failure is a natural fear, but as long as your basic needs are met (meaning a failure does not leave you without food, shelter, safety, or security), then failure is just a course correction toward success. If we can embrace failure, it inevitably reveals something valuable—learning more about ourselves. Think about it this way: If you never go after your goal because you are waiting for the right time or because you are afraid of failure, you have already failed. You'll never reach your goal. However, if you try and fail, what you learn from that failure levels you up for your next challenge. Real-world experience is your best education.

Worrying about what others think of you is also a natural instinct. It's said that these fears date back to hunter-gatherer societies where when someone returned from a hunt without a kill, they risked being kicked out of the tribe. Nowadays, however, the fear of what others think is often a misguided one. The simple truth: people are thinking about you much less than you think they are (often because they are too worried about what others are thinking of them), and people are willing to help you more often than you're probably giving them credit for.

The quicker we can identify these fears as imagined instead of real threats, the easier we can move past them and focus on what is truly important: our goal.

Problem: Fear
Solution: Identify the real fears and let go of imagined fears

*The problems we just addressed are the obstacles
this journal will help you overcome. Let's get to it.*

HOW THIS JOURNAL WORKS

STEP 1

Begin writing your list in 10 categories

STEP 2

Write your full list

STEP 3

Share your list

STEP 4

When you set out to achieve
a goal, start a "Before & After" page to
help you stay on track

STEP 5

Scan the QR code on page 198 for
more support with your goals

DOS & DON'TS
OF WRITING YOUR LIST

DON'TS	DOS
Prioritize love	Go on one new date per month
Get in shape	Run 5 miles twice per week
Travel more	Visit three new countries this year
Be healthier	Be vegetarian for 6 months
Read more	Read one book per month this year
Get my sales up	Close five deals per week for the next 3 months

QUICK TRICKS

Attach a timeline or a deadline
(even schedule time in your calendar)

Define your goal so that it's clear
whether you have achieved it or not

Name specific things and places

Be affirmative ("I will" instead of "try to")

Focus on actions, not intentions

STEP 1

10 CATEGORIES OF LIFE

When you think about common bucket list items, what comes to mind? Skydiving? Visiting the Great Barrier Reef? Maybe, bungy jumping or seeing the pyramids? Typically, your mind gravitates toward goals that fall into the "adventure and travel" bucket. While these are excellent items to list, they only cover one of the 10 categories that make up life.

In order to write a holistic list, you must reflect on all 10 Categories of Life. This ensures you've considered absolutely everything that might bring you joy and happiness and every dream, big or small.

In the next 10 pages, I outline the 10 Categories of Life and provide examples of items in each category. Hopefully, these examples will spark ideas for your own list. As you think about list items in each category, write them down on each page. This is the first step in your list writing process. Off you go!

1. TRAVEL & ADVENTURE

Since this is the category we typically think about when we think "bucket list," let's start here. Where have you always dreamed of going? What is the experience you'd absolutely love to do?

Thought Starters:
Walk the Great Wall of China
See my favorite band live
Learn to fly a biplane
Climb a 14,000 ft mountain
Eat my way across Italy
Visit the Picasso museum in Paris
Go skydiving with sharks (wait...)

One of my favorite Travel & Adventure list items: Learn to scuba dive

_____

_____

_____

_____

_____

_____

_____

_____

_____

_____

_____

_____

_____

_____

_____

2. PHYSICAL HEALTH

What goals do you have for your physical health? This could include positive lifestyle habits, exercise goals, or kicking bad habits.

Thought Starters:
Run a marathon
Only have X drinks a week
Walk 3 times per week
Get a personal trainer
Be vegetarian
Pick up tennis again
No screen time after 9pm

One of my favorite Physical Health list items: Reward myself after every workout

_____

_____

_____

_____

_____

_____

_____

_____

_____

_____

_____

_____

_____

_____

3. MATERIAL

It's okay to have material goals! What do you want to buy that would bring you true joy and happiness? It's important that the material things are not the "shoulds" that impress others but the things that spark joy within you. These goals can be big or small; they can also be for someone else.

Thought Starters:
Buy a sailboat
Save up for new skis
Become a homeowner
Surprise my kids with a new car
Buy flowers for myself once a month

One of my favorite Material list items: Buy a vintage Rolex

_____

_____

_____

_____

_____

_____

_____

_____

_____

_____

_____

_____

_____

_____

4. CREATIVE

Creativity is an often overlooked pillar of wellness. Don't forget to carve out time for your creative pursuits. When you are being creative, you are channeling a true version of yourself. It's not only fun, but also therapeutic.

Thought Starters:
Take a painting class
Write my book
Learn to play the violin
Take improv classes
Use my phone's camera to start learning photography
Start my YouTube channel

One of my favorite Creative list items: Take pottery classes

---

5. PROFESSIONAL

What goals do you have in your work life? This could be taking the next step in your career, creating a healthier work-life harmony, or taking that moonshot.

Thought Starters:
Become a more effective leader
Hit growth or sales goals
Ask for a promotion
Start my side hustle
No work after 8pm

One of my most memorable Professional list items: Make the jump into public speaking

---

---

6. FINANCIAL

What are your money-related goals? This could be investment benchmarks, income goals, or feeling financially free.

Thought Starters:
Send my kids to college
Become debt free
Make a donation
Earn $XXX per year
Build my portfolio to $XXX
Retire when I'm 50

One of my most helpful Financial list items: Find a financial advisor I trust

---

_____

_____

_____

_____

_____

_____

_____

_____

_____

_____

_____

_____

_____

_____

_____

_____

7. INTELLECTUAL

What goals do you have for your brain? This could be reading, learning a new skill, or following your curiosity to see where it takes you.

Thought Starters:
Read one book a month or each night before bed
Learn a new skill or take a class
Play chess once a week
Learn a new language

One of my favorite Intellectual list items: Have curiosity conversations with people in different fields of work

---

---

8. MENTAL HEALTH

How can you increase your emotional and spiritual wellbeing? This could include overcoming a fear, letting go of something, or finally facing the hard stuff you've buried deep inside.

Thought Starters:
Tell someone how I really feel
Learn to meditate or practice mindfulness
Embrace uncertainty
Start each day with a walk without my phone
Join a men's or women's group

One of my favorite Mental Health list items: Find a therapist I love to talk to

_____

_____

_____

_____

_____

_____

_____

_____

_____

_____

_____

_____

9. RELATIONSHIPS

This is all about the people you love: your partner, your friends, or your family. Perhaps you want to find love or meaningful relationships; these goals can also live here.

Thought Starters:
Prioritize finding romantic love
Spend more time with people who give me energy vs. take energy
Reconnect with someone I care about
Deepen the relationships that bring me the most joy
Date night twice per week
Find the one

One of my favorite Relationships list items: Surround myself with people that inspire me

_____

_____

_____

_____

_____

_____

_____

_____

_____

_____

_____

_____

_____

_____

_____

_____

10. GIVING

Spoiler Alert: these will probably be your most memorable list items. They may seem the least exciting but they will be the ones you remember at the end of your life.

Thought Starters:
Help someone I love pursue their dream
Recycle every piece of plastic I use
Take a mission trip with my kids
Help underprivileged youth
Take my mom to Ireland
Spend more time on the cause that means so much to me

One of my favorite Giving list items: Surprising a homeless man with his very first truck to start a landscaping business

_____

_____

_____

_____

_____

_____

_____

_____

_____

_____

_____

_____

_____

_____

STEP 2

YOUR LIST

Now it's time to build your full list. Take the list items that you wrote under your *10 Categories of Life* and write them again on your full list (next page). Once you've finished, take some time to add any more dreams and goals you have. Slow down enough to really think about what's important to you, not what's important to your friends or family or anyone else.

If you're having trouble thinking of more list items, that's okay. Instead of thinking, try feeling. What excites you? What gives you butterflies in your stomach just imagining it? What inspires curiosity? Key off of those feelings and keep writing down the things that stand out.

Remember, when you write down your dream you give it its first breath of life. You turn an idea into a project. You make something intangible tangible. A dream has a funny way of staying a dream, but a project has manageable steps toward a specific end. Writing down your dream is the first step in your project. Now, turn the page and start writing.

MY LIST

1. _____
2. _____
3. _____
4. _____
5. _____
6. _____
7. _____
8. _____
9. _____
10. _____
11. _____
12. _____
13. _____
14. _____
15. _____
16. _____
17. _____
18. _____
19. _____
20. _____
21. _____
22. _____
23. _____
24. _____
25. _____

26. _____

27. _____

28. _____

29. _____

30. _____

31. _____

32. _____

33. _____

34. _____

35. _____

36. _____

37. _____

38. _____

39. _____

40. _____

41. _____

42. _____

43. _____

44. _____

45. _____

46. _____

47. _____

48. _____

49. _____

50. _____

51. _____

52. _____

53. _____

54. _____

55. _____

56. _____

57. _____

58. _____

59. _____

60. _____

61. _____

62. _____

63. _____

64. _____

65. _____

66. _____

67. _____

68. _____

69. _____

70. _____

71. _____

72. _____

73. _____

74. _____

75. _____

76. _____

77. _____

78. _____

79. _____

80. _____

81. _____

82. _____

83. _____

84. _____

85. _____

86. _____

87. _____

88. _____

89. _____

90. _____

91. _____

92. _____

93. _____

94. _____

95. _____

96. _____

97. _____

98. _____

99. _____

100. _____

TOP 5 REGRETS OF THE DYING[2]

1.

"I wish I'd had the courage to live a life true to myself, not the life others expected of me"

2.

"I wish I hadn't worked so hard"

3.

"I wish I'd had the courage to express my feelings"

4.

"I wish I had stayed in touch with my friends"

5.

"I wish that I had let myself be happier"

*P.S. If these spark any new list ideas,
go back and add them to your list.*

STEP 3

SHARE YOUR LIST

1.

Write Down Your Top Goals
*Writing down your goals makes them tangible
and creates a reminder that they exist.*

2.

Take a Picture and Share It on Social Media
If you don't share you list, no one can help you.

3.

Tag Your Friends to Keep You Accountable
*You are 65% more likely to complete
a goal if you share your commitment to
it with somebody else.[3] Don't forget to
tag me @bennemtin :)*

In the following pages, write down your top goals and your accountability buddies who will help keep you on track along the way. Take a photo of your goal and share it on your social media to make a public commitment.

A good accountability buddy is someone who you feel comfortable sharing your goals with and who will encourage you to succeed. If you want to significantly increase your odds of success, send them a weekly progress report and ask them to check in with you to keep you accountable.

LIFE SHRINKS OR EXPANDS IN PROPORTION TO ONE'S COURAGE.

ANAIS NIN

BEFORE I DIE I WILL

Accountability Buddies:

"DREAMS MULTIPLY WHEN YOU SHARE THEM WITH THE WORLD."
—BEN NEMTIN

BEFORE I DIE I WILL

Accountability Buddies:

"DREAMS MULTIPLY WHEN YOU SHARE THEM WITH THE WORLD."
—BEN NEMTIN

BEFORE I DIE I WILL

Accountability Buddies:

"DREAMS MULTIPLY WHEN YOU SHARE THEM WITH THE WORLD."
—BEN NEMTIN

BEFORE I DIE I WILL

Accountability Buddies:

"DREAMS MULTIPLY WHEN YOU SHARE THEM WITH THE WORLD."
—BEN NEMTIN

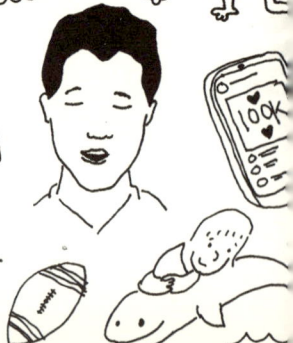

BEFORE I DIE I WILL

Accountability Buddies:

"DREAMS MULTIPLY WHEN YOU SHARE THEM WITH THE WORLD."
-BEN NEMTIN

YOUR BIG OPPORTUNITY MAY BE RIGHT WHERE YOU ARE NOW.

NAPOLEON HILL

STEP 4

BEFORE & AFTER

The following "Before & After" pages are designed to help you accomplish your list items. Write one list item that you want to work toward at the top of each page and begin the process. These exercises will help you break your goal into smaller steps, identify your fears, and build systems of accountability. Let's go!

LIST ITEM: _____

Write down the list item you want to accomplish.

If you feel stuck, there's a journaling section on page 170 to work through your thoughts.

BEFORE

This is important to me because:

_____
_____
_____
_____

My reward for completing this goal will be: _____

I will complete this by: My accountability buddy is:

_____   _____

3 things I can do in the next 48 hours: What's stopping me?

1. _____   _____
2. _____   _____
3. _____   _____

Additional small steps I can take to move forward:

_____
_____
_____

AFTER

Date completed: _____ ☐   How did it feel?

_____

What did I learn?   _____

_____   Can I help someone do this?

_____
_____   _____
_____   _____
_____   _____

LIST ITEM: _____

Write down the list item you want to accomplish.

If you feel stuck, there's a journaling section on page 170 to work through your thoughts.

BEFORE

This is important to me because:

_____

_____

_____

_____

My reward for completing this goal will be: _____

I will complete this by:

_____

My accountability buddy is:

_____

3 things I can do in the next 48 hours:

1. _____

2. _____

3. _____

What's stopping me?

_____

_____

_____

Additional small steps I can take to move forward:

_____

_____

_____

AFTER

Date completed: _____ ☐

How did it feel?

_____

What did I learn?

_____

_____

_____

_____

_____

Can I help someone do this?

_____

_____

LIST ITEM: _____

BEFORE

This is important to me because:

_____

_____

_____

_____

My reward for completing this goal will be: _____

I will complete this by: My accountability buddy is:

_____   _____

3 things I can do in the next 48 hours: What's stopping me?

1._____   _____

2._____   _____

3._____   _____

Additional small steps I can take to move forward:

_____

_____

_____

AFTER

Date completed: _____ ☐   How did it feel?

                                        _____

                                        _____

What did I learn?

_____   Can I help someone do this?

_____   _____

_____   _____

_____   _____

LIST ITEM: _____

BEFORE

This is important to me because:

_____

_____

_____

_____

My reward for completing this goal will be: _____

I will complete this by: My accountability buddy is:

_____   _____

3 things I can do in the next 48 hours: What's stopping me?

1. _____   _____

2. _____   _____

3. _____   _____

Additional small steps I can take to move forward:

_____

_____

_____

AFTER

Date completed: _____ ☐   How did it feel?

                                       _____

What did I learn?   _____

_____

_____   Can I help someone do this?

_____   _____

_____   _____

_____   _____

LIST ITEM: _____

BEFORE

This is important to me because:

_____

_____

_____

_____

My reward for completing this goal will be: _____

I will complete this by: My accountability buddy is:

_____   _____

3 things I can do in the next 48 hours: What's stopping me?

1. _____   _____

2. _____   _____

3. _____   _____

Additional small steps I can take to move forward:

_____

_____

_____

AFTER

Date completed: _____ ☐   How did it feel?

                                                     _____

What did I learn?   _____

_____   Can I help someone do this?

_____

_____   _____

_____   _____

LIST ITEM: _____

BEFORE

This is important to me because:

_____

_____

_____

_____

My reward for completing this goal will be: _____

I will complete this by: My accountability buddy is:

_____   _____

3 things I can do in the next 48 hours: What's stopping me?

1. _____   _____

2. _____   _____

3. _____   _____

Additional small steps I can take to move forward:

_____

_____

_____

AFTER

Date completed: _____ ☐   How did it feel?

                                            _____

What did I learn?   _____

_____

_____   Can I help someone do this?

_____   _____

_____   _____

LIST ITEM: _____

BEFORE

This is important to me because:

_____

_____

_____

_____

My reward for completing this goal will be: _____

I will complete this by: My accountability buddy is:

_____   _____

3 things I can do in the next 48 hours: What's stopping me?

1. _____   _____

2. _____   _____

3. _____   _____

Additional small steps I can take to move forward:

_____

_____

_____

AFTER

Date completed: _____ ☐   How did it feel?

                                            _____

What did I learn?   _____

_____   _____

_____   Can I help someone do this?

_____   _____

_____   _____

_____   _____

IF YOU WANT TO BE HAPPY, SET A GOAL THAT COMMANDS YOUR THOUGHTS, LIBERATES YOUR ENERGY, AND INSPIRES YOUR HOPES.

ANDREW CARNEGIE

LIST ITEM: _____

BEFORE

This is important to me because:

_____

_____

_____

_____

My reward for completing this goal will be: _____

I will complete this by: My accountability buddy is:

_____   _____

3 things I can do in the next 48 hours: What's stopping me?

1. _____   _____

2. _____   _____

3. _____   _____

Additional small steps I can take to move forward:

_____

_____

AFTER

Date completed: _____ ☐   How did it feel?

                                            _____

                                            _____

What did I learn?

_____   Can I help someone do this?

_____   _____

_____   _____

_____   _____

LIST ITEM: _____

BEFORE

This is important to me because:

_____

_____

_____

_____

My reward for completing this goal will be: _____

I will complete this by: My accountability buddy is:

_____   _____

3 things I can do in the next 48 hours: What's stopping me?

1. _____   _____

2. _____   _____

3. _____   _____

Additional small steps I can take to move forward:

_____

_____

_____

AFTER

Date completed: _____ ☐

What did I learn?

_____

_____

_____

_____

How did it feel?

_____

_____

Can I help someone do this?

_____

_____

LIST ITEM: _____

BEFORE

This is important to me because:

_____

_____

_____

_____

My reward for completing this goal will be: _____

I will complete this by: My accountability buddy is:

_____   _____

3 things I can do in the next 48 hours: What's stopping me?

1._____   _____

2._____   _____

3._____   _____

Additional small steps I can take to move forward:

_____

_____

_____

AFTER

Date completed: _____ ☐   How did it feel?

_____

What did I learn?   _____

_____   Can I help someone do this?

_____   _____

_____   _____

_____   _____

LIST ITEM: _____

BEFORE

This is important to me because:

_____

_____

_____

_____

My reward for completing this goal will be: _____

I will complete this by: My accountability buddy is:

_____   _____

3 things I can do in the next 48 hours: What's stopping me?

1. _____   _____

2. _____   _____

3. _____   _____

Additional small steps I can take to move forward:

_____

_____

_____

AFTER

Date completed: _____ ☐   How did it feel?

                                          _____

                                          _____

What did I learn?

_____   Can I help someone do this?

_____   _____

_____   _____

_____   _____

REMEMBER THAT WHEREVER YOUR HEART IS, THERE YOU WILL FIND YOUR TREASURE.

PAULO COELHO

LIST ITEM: _____

BEFORE

This is important to me because:

_____

_____

_____

_____

My reward for completing this goal will be: _____

I will complete this by: My accountability buddy is:

_____   _____

3 things I can do in the next 48 hours: What's stopping me?

1._____   _____

2._____   _____

3._____   _____

Additional small steps I can take to move forward:

_____

_____

_____

AFTER

Date completed: _____ ☐

What did I learn?

_____

_____

_____

_____

How did it feel?

_____

_____

Can I help someone do this?

_____

_____

_____

LIST ITEM: _____

BEFORE

This is important to me because:

_____

_____

_____

_____

My reward for completing this goal will be: _____

I will complete this by: My accountability buddy is:

_____   _____

3 things I can do in the next 48 hours: What's stopping me?

1. _____   _____

2. _____   _____

3. _____   _____

Additional small steps I can take to move forward:

_____

_____

_____

AFTER

Date completed: _____ ☐   How did it feel?

                                     _____

What did I learn?   _____

_____   _____

_____   Can I help someone do this?

_____   _____

_____   _____

_____   _____

LIST ITEM: _____

BEFORE

This is important to me because:

_____

_____

_____

_____

My reward for completing this goal will be: _____

I will complete this by: My accountability buddy is:

_____   _____

3 things I can do in the next 48 hours: What's stopping me?

1. _____

2. _____   _____

3. _____   _____

Additional small steps I can take to move forward:

_____

_____

_____

AFTER

Date completed: _____ ☐   How did it feel?

                                            _____

What did I learn?   _____

_____

_____   Can I help someone do this?

_____   _____

_____   _____

LIST ITEM: _____

BEFORE

This is important to me because:

_____

_____

_____

_____

My reward for completing this goal will be: _____

I will complete this by: My accountability buddy is:

_____   _____

3 things I can do in the next 48 hours: What's stopping me?

1. _____   _____

2. _____   _____

3. _____   _____

Additional small steps I can take to move forward:

_____

_____

_____

AFTER

Date completed: _____ ☐   How did it feel?

                                            _____

What did I learn?   _____

_____

_____   Can I help someone do this?

_____   _____

_____   _____

LIST ITEM: _____

BEFORE

This is important to me because:

_____

_____

_____

_____

My reward for completing this goal will be: _____

I will complete this by: My accountability buddy is:

_____   _____

3 things I can do in the next 48 hours: What's stopping me?

1. _____   _____

2. _____   _____

3. _____   _____

Additional small steps I can take to move forward:

_____

_____

_____

AFTER

Date completed: _____ ☐   How did it feel?

                                            _____

What did I learn?   _____

_____   _____

_____   Can I help someone do this?

_____   _____

_____   _____

_____   _____

LIST ITEM: _____

BEFORE

This is important to me because:

_____

_____

_____

_____

My reward for completing this goal will be: _____

I will complete this by: My accountability buddy is:

_____   _____

3 things I can do in the next 48 hours: What's stopping me?

1._____   _____

2._____   _____

3._____   _____

Additional small steps I can take to move forward:

_____

_____

_____

AFTER

Date completed: _____ ☐   How did it feel?

                                        _____

What did I learn?   _____

_____

_____   Can I help someone do this?

_____   _____

_____   _____

NEVER BE LIMITED BY OTHER PEOPLE'S LIMITED IMAGINATIONS.

MAE JEMISON

LIST ITEM: _____

BEFORE

This is important to me because:

_____

_____

_____

_____

My reward for completing this goal will be: _____

I will complete this by: My accountability buddy is:

_____   _____

3 things I can do in the next 48 hours: What's stopping me?

1._____   _____

2._____   _____

3._____   _____

Additional small steps I can take to move forward:

_____

_____

_____

AFTER

Date completed: _____ ☐   How did it feel?

                                        _____

                                        _____

What did I learn?

                                        Can I help someone do this?

_____

_____   _____

_____   _____

_____   _____

LIST ITEM: _____

BEFORE

This is important to me because:

_____

_____

_____

_____

My reward for completing this goal will be: _____

I will complete this by: My accountability buddy is:

_____   _____

3 things I can do in the next 48 hours: What's stopping me?

1._____   _____

2._____   _____

3._____   _____

Additional small steps I can take to move forward:

_____

_____

_____

AFTER

Date completed: _____ ☐   How did it feel?

                                            _____

What did I learn?   _____

_____   Can I help someone do this?

_____   _____

_____   _____

_____   _____

LIST ITEM: _____

BEFORE

This is important to me because:

_____

_____

_____

_____

My reward for completing this goal will be: _____

I will complete this by: My accountability buddy is:

_____   _____

3 things I can do in the next 48 hours: What's stopping me?

1. _____   _____

2. _____   _____

3. _____   _____

Additional small steps I can take to move forward:

_____

_____

_____

AFTER

Date completed: _____ ☐   How did it feel?

                                       _____

What did I learn?   _____

_____   _____

_____   Can I help someone do this?

_____   _____

_____   _____

_____   _____

LIST ITEM: _____

BEFORE

This is important to me because:

_____

_____

_____

_____

My reward for completing this goal will be: _____

I will complete this by: My accountability buddy is:

_____   _____

3 things I can do in the next 48 hours: What's stopping me?

1._____   _____

2._____   _____

3._____   _____

Additional small steps I can take to move forward:

_____

_____

_____

AFTER

Date completed: _____ ☐   How did it feel?

                                            _____

                                            _____

What did I learn?

_____   Can I help someone do this?

_____   _____

_____   _____

_____

THE BEST PLACE TO FIND A HELPING HAND IS AT THE END OF YOUR OWN ARM.

SWEDISH PROVERB

LIST ITEM: _____

BEFORE

This is important to me because:

_____

_____

_____

_____

My reward for completing this goal will be: _____

I will complete this by: My accountability buddy is:

_____   _____

3 things I can do in the next 48 hours: What's stopping me?

1._____   _____

2._____   _____

3._____   _____

Additional small steps I can take to move forward:

_____

_____

_____

AFTER

Date completed: _____ ☐   How did it feel?

                                             _____

What did I learn?   _____

_____   Can I help someone do this?

_____   _____

_____   _____

_____   _____

LIST ITEM: _____

BEFORE

This is important to me because:

_____

_____

_____

_____

My reward for completing this goal will be: _____

I will complete this by: My accountability buddy is:

_____   _____

3 things I can do in the next 48 hours: What's stopping me?

1. _____   _____

2. _____   _____

3. _____   _____

Additional small steps I can take to move forward:

_____

_____

_____

AFTER

Date completed: _____ ☐   How did it feel?

                                         _____

                                         _____

What did I learn?

_____   Can I help someone do this?

_____

_____   _____

_____   _____

LIST ITEM: _____

BEFORE

This is important to me because:

_____

_____

_____

_____

My reward for completing this goal will be: _____

I will complete this by: My accountability buddy is:

_____   _____

3 things I can do in the next 48 hours: What's stopping me?

1. _____   _____

2. _____   _____

3. _____   _____

Additional small steps I can take to move forward:

_____

_____

_____

AFTER

Date completed: _____ ☐   How did it feel?

                                         _____

What did I learn?   _____

_____

_____   Can I help someone do this?

_____   _____

_____   _____

LIST ITEM: _____

BEFORE

This is important to me because:

_____

_____

_____

_____

My reward for completing this goal will be: _____

I will complete this by: My accountability buddy is:

_____   _____

3 things I can do in the next 48 hours: What's stopping me?

1. _____   _____

2. _____   _____

3. _____   _____

Additional small steps I can take to move forward:

_____

_____

_____

AFTER

Date completed: _____ ☐   How did it feel?

                                            _____

What did I learn?   _____

_____   _____

_____   Can I help someone do this?

_____   _____

_____   _____

LIST ITEM: _____

BEFORE

This is important to me because:

_____

_____

_____

_____

My reward for completing this goal will be: _____

I will complete this by: My accountability buddy is:

_____   _____

3 things I can do in the next 48 hours: What's stopping me?

1. _____

2. _____   _____

3. _____   _____

_____

Additional small steps I can take to move forward:

_____

_____

_____

AFTER

Date completed: _____ ☐   How did it feel?

_____

What did I learn?   _____

_____   _____

_____   Can I help someone do this?

_____   _____

_____   _____

_____   _____

LIST ITEM: _____

BEFORE

This is important to me because:

_____

_____

_____

_____

My reward for completing this goal will be: _____

I will complete this by: My accountability buddy is:

_____   _____

3 things I can do in the next 48 hours: What's stopping me?

1._____   _____

2._____   _____

3._____   _____

Additional small steps I can take to move forward:

_____

_____

_____

AFTER

Date completed: _____ ☐   How did it feel?

                                              _____

What did I learn?   _____

_____

_____   Can I help someone do this?

_____   _____

_____   _____

EXPERIENCE IS SIMPLY THE NAME WE GIVE OUR MISTAKES.

OSCAR WILDE

LIST ITEM: _____

BEFORE

This is important to me because:

_____

_____

_____

_____

My reward for completing this goal will be: _____

I will complete this by: My accountability buddy is:

_____   _____

3 things I can do in the next 48 hours: What's stopping me?

1._____   _____

2._____   _____

3._____   _____

Additional small steps I can take to move forward:

_____

_____

_____

AFTER

Date completed: _____ ☐   How did it feel?

                                            _____

What did I learn?   _____

_____

_____   Can I help someone do this?

_____   _____

_____   _____

LIST ITEM: _____

BEFORE

This is important to me because:

_____

_____

_____

_____

My reward for completing this goal will be: _____

I will complete this by: My accountability buddy is:

_____   _____

3 things I can do in the next 48 hours: What's stopping me?

1. _____   _____

2. _____   _____

3. _____   _____

Additional small steps I can take to move forward:

_____

_____

_____

AFTER

Date completed: _____ ☐

What did I learn?

_____

_____

_____

_____

How did it feel?

_____

_____

Can I help someone do this?

_____

_____

_____

LIST ITEM: _____

BEFORE

This is important to me because:

_____

_____

_____

_____

My reward for completing this goal will be: _____

I will complete this by: My accountability buddy is:

_____   _____

3 things I can do in the next 48 hours: What's stopping me?

1. _____   _____

2. _____   _____

3. _____   _____

Additional small steps I can take to move forward:

_____

_____

_____

AFTER

Date completed: _____ ☐   How did it feel?

                                        _____

What did I learn?   _____

_____   Can I help someone do this?

_____   _____

_____   _____

_____   _____

LIST ITEM: _____

BEFORE

This is important to me because:

_____

_____

_____

_____

My reward for completing this goal will be: _____

I will complete this by: My accountability buddy is:

_____   _____

3 things I can do in the next 48 hours: What's stopping me?

1. _____   _____

2. _____   _____

3. _____   _____

Additional small steps I can take to move forward:

_____

_____

_____

AFTER

Date completed: _____ ☐   How did it feel?

_____

What did I learn?   _____

_____

_____   Can I help someone do this?

_____   _____

_____   _____

_____   _____

THE DEATH OF A DREAM IS THE DAY THAT YOU STOP BELIEVING IN THE WORK IT TAKES TO GET THERE.

CHRIS BURKMENN

LIST ITEM: _____

BEFORE

This is important to me because:

_____

_____

_____

_____

My reward for completing this goal will be: _____

I will complete this by: My accountability buddy is:

_____   _____

3 things I can do in the next 48 hours: What's stopping me?

1._____   _____

2._____   _____

3._____   _____

Additional small steps I can take to move forward:

_____

_____

_____

AFTER

Date completed: _____ ☐   How did it feel?

                                    _____

What did I learn?   _____

_____   _____

_____   Can I help someone do this?

_____   _____

_____   _____

LIST ITEM: _____

BEFORE

This is important to me because:

_____

_____

_____

_____

My reward for completing this goal will be: _____

I will complete this by: My accountability buddy is:

_____   _____

3 things I can do in the next 48 hours: What's stopping me?

1. _____   _____

2. _____   _____

3. _____   _____

Additional small steps I can take to move forward:

_____

_____

_____

AFTER

Date completed: _____ ☐   How did it feel?

                                            _____

What did I learn?   _____

_____   Can I help someone do this?

_____   _____

_____   _____

_____   _____

LIST ITEM: _____

BEFORE

This is important to me because:

_____

_____

_____

_____

My reward for completing this goal will be: _____

I will complete this by: My accountability buddy is:

_____   _____

3 things I can do in the next 48 hours: What's stopping me?

1. _____   _____

2. _____   _____

3. _____   _____

Additional small steps I can take to move forward:

_____

_____

_____

AFTER

Date completed: _____ ☐

How did it feel?

_____

_____

What did I learn?

_____   _____

_____   Can I help someone do this?

_____   _____

_____   _____

LIST ITEM: _____

BEFORE

This is important to me because:

_____

_____

_____

_____

My reward for completing this goal will be: _____

I will complete this by: My accountability buddy is:

_____   _____

3 things I can do in the next 48 hours: What's stopping me?

1. _____   _____

2. _____   _____

3. _____   _____

Additional small steps I can take to move forward:

_____

_____

_____

AFTER

Date completed: _____ ☐   How did it feel?

                                             _____

What did I learn?   _____

_____   Can I help someone do this?

_____

_____   _____

_____   _____

                                             _____

LIST ITEM: _____

BEFORE

This is important to me because:

_____

_____

_____

_____

My reward for completing this goal will be: _____

I will complete this by: My accountability buddy is:

_____   _____

3 things I can do in the next 48 hours: What's stopping me?

1. _____   _____

2. _____   _____

3. _____   _____

Additional small steps I can take to move forward:

_____

_____

_____

AFTER

Date completed: _____ ☐   How did it feel?

                                            _____

What did I learn?   _____

_____

_____   Can I help someone do this?

_____   _____

_____   _____

LIST ITEM: _____

BEFORE

This is important to me because:

_____

_____

_____

_____

My reward for completing this goal will be: _____

I will complete this by: My accountability buddy is:

_____   _____

3 things I can do in the next 48 hours: What's stopping me?

1. _____   _____

2. _____   _____

3. _____   _____

Additional small steps I can take to move forward:

_____

_____

_____

AFTER

Date completed: _____ ☐   How did it feel?

                                           _____

What did I learn?   _____

_____

_____   Can I help someone do this?

_____   _____

_____   _____

_____   _____

YOU LIVE LONGER ONCE YOU REALIZE THAT ANY TIME SPENT BEING UNHAPPY IS WASTED.

RUTH E. RENKL

LIST ITEM: _____

BEFORE

This is important to me because:

_____

_____

_____

_____

My reward for completing this goal will be: _____

I will complete this by: My accountability buddy is:

_____   _____

3 things I can do in the next 48 hours: What's stopping me?

1._____   _____

2._____   _____

3._____   _____

Additional small steps I can take to move forward:

_____

_____

_____

AFTER

Date completed: _____ ☐   How did it feel?

                                            _____

What did I learn?   _____

_____   Can I help someone do this?

_____   _____

_____   _____

_____   _____

LIST ITEM: _____

BEFORE

This is important to me because:

_____

_____

_____

_____

My reward for completing this goal will be: _____

I will complete this by: My accountability buddy is:

_____   _____

3 things I can do in the next 48 hours: What's stopping me?

1._____   _____

2._____   _____

3._____   _____

Additional small steps I can take to move forward:

_____

_____

_____

AFTER

Date completed: _____ ☐   How did it feel?

                                            _____

What did I learn?   _____

_____   _____

_____   Can I help someone do this?

_____   _____

_____   _____

_____   _____

LIST ITEM: _____

BEFORE

This is important to me because:

_____

_____

_____

_____

My reward for completing this goal will be: _____

I will complete this by: My accountability buddy is:

_____   _____

3 things I can do in the next 48 hours: What's stopping me?

1. _____   _____

2. _____   _____

3. _____   _____

Additional small steps I can take to move forward:

_____

_____

_____

AFTER

Date completed: _____ ☐   How did it feel?

                                            _____

What did I learn?   _____

_____   _____

_____   Can I help someone do this?

_____   _____

_____   _____

_____   _____

LIST ITEM: _____

BEFORE

This is important to me because:

_____

_____

_____

_____

My reward for completing this goal will be: _____

I will complete this by: My accountability buddy is:

_____   _____

3 things I can do in the next 48 hours: What's stopping me?

1. _____   _____

2. _____   _____

3. _____   _____

Additional small steps I can take to move forward:

_____

_____

_____

AFTER

Date completed: _____ ☐

What did I learn?

_____

_____

_____

_____

How did it feel?

_____

_____

Can I help someone do this?

_____

_____

OFTEN WHEN YOU THINK YOU'RE AT THE END OF SOMETHING, YOU'RE AT THE BEGINNING OF SOMETHING ELSE.

FRED ROGERS

LIST ITEM: _____

BEFORE

This is important to me because:

_____

_____

_____

_____

My reward for completing this goal will be: _____

I will complete this by: My accountability buddy is:

_____   _____

3 things I can do in the next 48 hours: What's stopping me?

1. _____   _____

2. _____   _____

3. _____   _____

Additional small steps I can take to move forward:

_____

_____

_____

AFTER

Date completed: _____ ☐   How did it feel?

                                                 _____

What did I learn?   _____

_____   _____

_____   Can I help someone do this?

_____   _____

_____   _____

LIST ITEM: _____

BEFORE

This is important to me because:

_____
_____
_____
_____

My reward for completing this goal will be: _____

I will complete this by:

_____

3 things I can do in the next 48 hours:

1. _____
2. _____
3. _____

Additional small steps I can take to move forward:

_____
_____
_____

My accountability buddy is:

_____

What's stopping me?

_____
_____
_____

AFTER

Date completed: _____ ☐

What did I learn?

_____
_____
_____
_____
_____

How did it feel?

_____
_____

Can I help someone do this?

_____
_____

LIST ITEM: _____

BEFORE

This is important to me because:

_____

_____

_____

_____

My reward for completing this goal will be: _____

I will complete this by: My accountability buddy is:

_____   _____

3 things I can do in the next 48 hours: What's stopping me?

1._____   _____

2._____   _____

3._____   _____

Additional small steps I can take to move forward:

_____

_____

_____

AFTER

Date completed: _____ ☐   How did it feel?

                                            _____

What did I learn?   _____

_____   Can I help someone do this?

_____   _____

_____   _____

_____   _____

_____   _____

LIST ITEM: _____

BEFORE

This is important to me because:

_____
_____
_____
_____

My reward for completing this goal will be: _____

I will complete this by: My accountability buddy is:

_____   _____

3 things I can do in the next 48 hours: What's stopping me?

1._____   _____
2._____
3._____   _____

Additional small steps I can take to move forward:

_____
_____
_____

AFTER

Date completed: _____ ☐   How did it feel?

                                      _____

What did I learn?   _____

_____   Can I help someone do this?

_____   _____

_____   _____

LIST ITEM: _____

BEFORE

This is important to me because:

_____

_____

_____

_____

My reward for completing this goal will be: _____

I will complete this by: My accountability buddy is:

_____   _____

3 things I can do in the next 48 hours: What's stopping me?

1._____   _____

2._____   _____

3._____   _____

Additional small steps I can take to move forward:

_____

_____

_____

AFTER

Date completed: _____ ☐   How did it feel?

                                            _____

What did I learn?   _____

_____   Can I help someone do this?

_____   _____

_____   _____

_____   _____

LIST ITEM: _____

BEFORE

This is important to me because:

_____

_____

_____

_____

My reward for completing this goal will be: _____

I will complete this by: My accountability buddy is:

_____   _____

3 things I can do in the next 48 hours: What's stopping me?

1._____   _____

2._____   _____

3._____   _____

Additional small steps I can take to move forward:

_____

_____

_____

AFTER

Date completed: _____ ☐   How did it feel?

                                        _____

What did I learn?   _____

_____

_____   Can I help someone do this?

_____   _____

_____   _____

FORGET ALL THE REASONS WHY IT WON'T WORK AND BELIEVE THE ONE REASON WHY IT WILL.

ZIAD ABDELNOUR

LIST ITEM: _____

BEFORE

This is important to me because:

_____

_____

_____

_____

My reward for completing this goal will be: _____

I will complete this by: My accountability buddy is:

_____   _____

3 things I can do in the next 48 hours: What's stopping me?

1. _____   _____

2. _____   _____

3. _____   _____

Additional small steps I can take to move forward:

_____

_____

_____

AFTER

Date completed: _____ ☐   How did it feel?

                                        _____

What did I learn?   _____

_____   Can I help someone do this?

_____

_____   _____

_____   _____

LIST ITEM: _____

BEFORE

This is important to me because:

_____
_____
_____
_____

My reward for completing this goal will be: _____

I will complete this by: My accountability buddy is:

_____   _____

3 things I can do in the next 48 hours: What's stopping me?

1. _____   _____

2. _____   _____

3. _____   _____

Additional small steps I can take to move forward:

_____
_____
_____

AFTER

Date completed: _____ ☐   How did it feel?

                                  _____

                                  _____

What did I learn?

_____   Can I help someone do this?

_____   _____

_____   _____

_____   _____

LIST ITEM: _____

BEFORE

This is important to me because:

_____

_____

_____

_____

My reward for completing this goal will be: _____

I will complete this by: My accountability buddy is:

_____   _____

3 things I can do in the next 48 hours: What's stopping me?

1._____   _____

2._____   _____

3._____   _____

Additional small steps I can take to move forward:

_____

_____

_____

AFTER

Date completed: _____ ☐   How did it feel?

                                            _____

What did I learn?   _____

_____   _____

_____   Can I help someone do this?

_____   _____

_____   _____

_____   _____

LIST ITEM: _____

BEFORE

This is important to me because:

_____

_____

_____

_____

My reward for completing this goal will be: _____

I will complete this by: My accountability buddy is:

_____   _____

3 things I can do in the next 48 hours: What's stopping me?

1. _____   _____

2. _____   _____

3. _____   _____

Additional small steps I can take to move forward:

_____

_____

_____

AFTER

Date completed: _____ ☐   How did it feel?

                                       _____

What did I learn?   _____

_____   Can I help someone do this?

_____   _____

_____   _____

_____   _____

DON'T LET SOMEONE WHO GAVE UP ON THEIR DREAMS TALK YOU OUT OF GOING AFTER YOURS.

ZIG ZIGLAR

LIST ITEM: _____

BEFORE

This is important to me because:

_____

_____

_____

_____

My reward for completing this goal will be: _____

I will complete this by: My accountability buddy is:

_____   _____

3 things I can do in the next 48 hours: What's stopping me?

1._____   _____

2._____   _____

3._____   _____

Additional small steps I can take to move forward:

_____

_____

_____

AFTER

Date completed: _____ ☐   How did it feel?

_____

What did I learn?   _____

_____   _____

_____   Can I help someone do this?

_____   _____

_____   _____

_____   _____

LIST ITEM: _____

BEFORE

This is important to me because:

_____

_____

_____

_____

My reward for completing this goal will be: _____

I will complete this by: My accountability buddy is:

_____   _____

3 things I can do in the next 48 hours: What's stopping me?

1. _____   _____

2. _____   _____

3. _____   _____

Additional small steps I can take to move forward:

_____

_____

_____

AFTER

Date completed: _____ ☐   How did it feel?

                                            _____

                                            _____

What did I learn?

_____   _____

_____   Can I help someone do this?

_____   _____

_____   _____

LIST ITEM: _____

BEFORE

This is important to me because:

_____

_____

_____

_____

My reward for completing this goal will be: _____

I will complete this by: My accountability buddy is:

_____   _____

3 things I can do in the next 48 hours: What's stopping me?

1. _____   _____

2. _____   _____

3. _____   _____

Additional small steps I can take to move forward:

_____

_____

_____

AFTER

Date completed: _____ ☐

What did I learn?

_____

_____

_____

_____

How did it feel?

_____

_____

Can I help someone do this?

_____

_____

LIST ITEM: _____

BEFORE

This is important to me because:

_____

_____

_____

_____

My reward for completing this goal will be: _____

I will complete this by: My accountability buddy is:

_____   _____

3 things I can do in the next 48 hours: What's stopping me?

1. _____   _____

2. _____   _____

3. _____   _____

Additional small steps I can take to move forward:

_____

_____

_____

AFTER

Date completed: _____ ☐   How did it feel?

                                         _____

What did I learn?   _____

_____   _____

_____   Can I help someone do this?

_____   _____

_____   _____

_____   _____

LIST ITEM: _____

BEFORE

This is important to me because:

_____

_____

_____

_____

My reward for completing this goal will be: _____

I will complete this by: My accountability buddy is:

_____   _____

3 things I can do in the next 48 hours: What's stopping me?

1. _____   _____

2. _____   _____

3. _____   _____

Additional small steps I can take to move forward:

_____

_____

_____

AFTER

Date completed: _____ ☐

What did I learn?

_____

_____

_____

_____

How did it feel?

_____

_____

Can I help someone do this?

_____

_____

LIST ITEM: _____

BEFORE

This is important to me because:

_____

_____

_____

_____

My reward for completing this goal will be: _____

I will complete this by: My accountability buddy is:

_____   _____

3 things I can do in the next 48 hours: What's stopping me?

1._____   _____

2._____   _____

3. _____   _____

Additional small steps I can take to move forward:

_____

_____

_____

AFTER

Date completed: _____ ☐   How did it feel?

                                           _____

What did I learn?   _____

_____

_____   Can I help someone do this?

_____   _____

_____   _____

KINDNESS IS MORE IMPORTANT THAN WISDOM, AND THE RECOGNITION OF THIS IS THE BEGINNING OF WISDOM.

THEODORE ISAAC RUBIN

LIST ITEM: _____

BEFORE

This is important to me because:

_____

_____

_____

_____

My reward for completing this goal will be: _____

I will complete this by:

_____

My accountability buddy is:

_____

3 things I can do in the next 48 hours:

1. _____

2. _____

3. _____

What's stopping me?

_____

_____

_____

Additional small steps I can take to move forward:

_____

_____

_____

AFTER

Date completed: _____ ☐

What did I learn?

_____

_____

_____

_____

How did it feel?

_____

_____

_____

Can I help someone do this?

_____

_____

LIST ITEM: _____

BEFORE

This is important to me because:

_____

_____

_____

_____

My reward for completing this goal will be: _____

I will complete this by: My accountability buddy is:

_____   _____

3 things I can do in the next 48 hours: What's stopping me?

1. _____   _____

2. _____   _____

3. _____   _____

Additional small steps I can take to move forward:

_____

_____

_____

AFTER

Date completed: _____ ☐   How did it feel?

                                            _____

What did I learn?   _____

_____

_____   Can I help someone do this?

_____   _____

_____   _____

LIST ITEM: _____

BEFORE

This is important to me because:

_____

_____

_____

_____

My reward for completing this goal will be: _____

I will complete this by: My accountability buddy is:

_____   _____

3 things I can do in the next 48 hours: What's stopping me?

1. _____   _____

2. _____   _____

3. _____   _____

Additional small steps I can take to move forward:

_____

_____

_____

AFTER

Date completed: _____ ☐   How did it feel?

                                        _____

                                        _____

What did I learn?

_____

_____   Can I help someone do this?

_____   _____

_____   _____

LIST ITEM: _____

BEFORE

This is important to me because:

_____

_____

_____

_____

My reward for completing this goal will be: _____

I will complete this by: My accountability buddy is:

_____   _____

3 things I can do in the next 48 hours: What's stopping me?

1. _____   _____

2. _____   _____

3. _____   _____

Additional small steps I can take to move forward:

_____

_____

_____

AFTER

Date completed: _____ ☐   How did it feel?

                                            _____

What did I learn?   _____

_____   _____

_____   Can I help someone do this?

_____   _____

_____   _____

ONE DAY YOU WILL WAKE UP AND THERE WON'T BE ANY MORE TIME TO DO THE THINGS YOU'VE ALWAYS WANTED. DO IT NOW.

PAULO COELHO

LIST ITEM: _____

BEFORE

This is important to me because:

_____

_____

_____

_____

My reward for completing this goal will be: _____

I will complete this by: My accountability buddy is:

_____   _____

3 things I can do in the next 48 hours: What's stopping me?

1. _____   _____

2. _____   _____

3. _____   _____

Additional small steps I can take to move forward:

_____

_____

_____

AFTER

Date completed: _____ ☐   How did it feel?

                                          _____

What did I learn?   _____

_____

_____   Can I help someone do this?

_____   _____

_____   _____

LIST ITEM: _____

BEFORE

This is important to me because:

_____

_____

_____

_____

My reward for completing this goal will be: _____

I will complete this by: My accountability buddy is:

_____   _____

3 things I can do in the next 48 hours: What's stopping me?

1._____   _____

2._____   _____

3._____   _____

Additional small steps I can take to move forward:

_____

_____

_____

AFTER

Date completed: _____ ☐   How did it feel?

                                            _____

What did I learn?   _____

_____

_____   Can I help someone do this?

_____   _____

_____   _____

LIST ITEM: _____

BEFORE

This is important to me because:

_____

_____

_____

_____

My reward for completing this goal will be: _____

I will complete this by: My accountability buddy is:

_____   _____

3 things I can do in the next 48 hours: What's stopping me?

1. _____   _____

2. _____   _____

3. _____   _____

Additional small steps I can take to move forward:

_____

_____

_____

AFTER

Date completed: _____ ☐

What did I learn?

_____

_____

_____

_____

How did it feel?

_____

_____

Can I help someone do this?

_____

_____

LIST ITEM: _____

BEFORE

This is important to me because:

_____

_____

_____

_____

My reward for completing this goal will be: _____

I will complete this by: My accountability buddy is:

_____   _____

3 things I can do in the next 48 hours: What's stopping me?

1._____   _____

2._____   _____

3._____   _____

Additional small steps I can take to move forward:

_____

_____

_____

AFTER

Date completed: _____ ☐   How did it feel?

                                             _____

What did I learn?   _____

_____   _____

_____   Can I help someone do this?

_____   _____

_____   _____

LIST ITEM: _____

BEFORE

This is important to me because:

_____

_____

_____

_____

My reward for completing this goal will be: _____

I will complete this by: My accountability buddy is:

_____   _____

3 things I can do in the next 48 hours: What's stopping me?

1._____   _____

2._____   _____

3._____   _____

Additional small steps I can take to move forward:

_____

_____

_____

AFTER

Date completed: _____ ☐   How did it feel?

                                            _____

What did I learn?   _____

_____

_____   Can I help someone do this?

_____   _____

_____   _____

LIST ITEM: _____

BEFORE

This is important to me because:

_____

_____

_____

_____

My reward for completing this goal will be: _____

I will complete this by:

_____

3 things I can do in the next 48 hours:

1. _____

2. _____

3. _____

My accountability buddy is:

_____

What's stopping me?

_____

_____

_____

Additional small steps I can take to move forward:

_____

_____

_____

AFTER

Date completed: _____ ☐

What did I learn?

_____

_____

_____

_____

How did it feel?

_____

_____

Can I help someone do this?

_____

_____

_____

I AM NO LONGER ACCEPTING THE THINGS I CANNOT CHANGE. I AM CHANGING THE THINGS I CANNOT ACCEPT.

ANGELA DAVIS

LIST ITEM: _____

BEFORE

This is important to me because:

_____

_____

_____

_____

My reward for completing this goal will be: _____

I will complete this by: My accountability buddy is:

_____   _____

3 things I can do in the next 48 hours: What's stopping me?

1. _____   _____

2. _____   _____

3. _____   _____

Additional small steps I can take to move forward:

_____

_____

_____

AFTER

Date completed: _____ ☐   How did it feel?

_____

What did I learn?   _____

_____   _____

_____   Can I help someone do this?

_____   _____

_____   _____

LIST ITEM: _____

BEFORE

This is important to me because:

_____

_____

_____

_____

My reward for completing this goal will be: _____

I will complete this by: My accountability buddy is:

_____   _____

3 things I can do in the next 48 hours: What's stopping me?

1. _____   _____

2. _____   _____

3. _____   _____

Additional small steps I can take to move forward:

_____

_____

_____

AFTER

Date completed: _____ ☐   How did it feel?

                                            _____

What did I learn?   _____

_____

_____   Can I help someone do this?

_____   _____

_____   _____

LIST ITEM: _____

BEFORE

This is important to me because:

_____

_____

_____

_____

My reward for completing this goal will be: _____

I will complete this by: My accountability buddy is:

_____   _____

3 things I can do in the next 48 hours: What's stopping me?

1. _____   _____

2. _____   _____

3. _____   _____

Additional small steps I can take to move forward:

_____

_____

_____

AFTER

Date completed: _____ ☐   How did it feel?

_____

What did I learn?   _____

_____

_____   Can I help someone do this?

_____   _____

_____   _____

_____   _____

LIST ITEM: _____

BEFORE

This is important to me because:

_____

_____

_____

_____

My reward for completing this goal will be: _____

I will complete this by: My accountability buddy is:

_____   _____

3 things I can do in the next 48 hours: What's stopping me?

1. _____   _____

2. _____   _____

3. _____   _____

Additional small steps I can take to move forward:

_____

_____

_____

AFTER

Date completed: _____ ☐   How did it feel?

                                            _____

What did I learn?   _____

_____   Can I help someone do this?

_____

_____   _____

_____   _____

ONE WHO MAKES NO MISTAKES, MAKES NOTHING AT ALL.

GIACOMO CASANOVA

LIST ITEM: _____

BEFORE

This is important to me because:

_____

_____

_____

_____

My reward for completing this goal will be: _____

I will complete this by: My accountability buddy is:

_____   _____

3 things I can do in the next 48 hours: What's stopping me?

1. _____   _____

2. _____   _____

3. _____   _____

Additional small steps I can take to move forward:

_____

_____

_____

AFTER

Date completed: _____ ☐   How did it feel?

                                            _____

What did I learn?   _____

_____

_____   Can I help someone do this?

_____   _____

_____   _____

LIST ITEM: _____

BEFORE

This is important to me because:

_____

_____

_____

_____

My reward for completing this goal will be: _____

I will complete this by: My accountability buddy is:

_____   _____

3 things I can do in the next 48 hours: What's stopping me?

1. _____   _____

2. _____   _____

3. _____   _____

Additional small steps I can take to move forward:

_____

_____

_____

AFTER

Date completed: _____ ☐   How did it feel?

_____

What did I learn?   _____

_____

_____   Can I help someone do this?

_____

_____   _____

_____   _____

LIST ITEM: _____

BEFORE

This is important to me because:

_____

_____

_____

_____

My reward for completing this goal will be: _____

I will complete this by: My accountability buddy is:

_____   _____

3 things I can do in the next 48 hours: What's stopping me?

1. _____   _____

2. _____   _____

3. _____   _____

Additional small steps I can take to move forward:

_____

_____

_____

AFTER

Date completed: _____ ☐

How did it feel?

_____

_____

What did I learn?

_____

_____   Can I help someone do this?

_____   _____

_____   _____

LIST ITEM: _____

BEFORE

This is important to me because:

_____

_____

_____

_____

My reward for completing this goal will be: _____

I will complete this by: My accountability buddy is:

_____   _____

3 things I can do in the next 48 hours: What's stopping me?

1._____   _____

2._____   _____

3.   _____
 _____

Additional small steps I can take to move forward:

_____

_____

_____

AFTER

Date completed: _____ ☐   How did it feel?

                                            _____

What did I learn?   _____

_____   Can I help someone do this?

_____

_____   _____

_____   _____

_____   _____

LIST ITEM: _____

BEFORE

This is important to me because:

_____

_____

_____

_____

My reward for completing this goal will be: _____

I will complete this by: My accountability buddy is:

_____   _____

3 things I can do in the next 48 hours: What's stopping me?

1. _____   _____

2. _____   _____

3. _____   _____

Additional small steps I can take to move forward:

_____

_____

_____

AFTER

Date completed: _____ ☐

How did it feel?

_____

What did I learn?

_____

_____   Can I help someone do this?

_____   _____

_____   _____

LIST ITEM: _____

BEFORE

This is important to me because:

_____

_____

_____

_____

My reward for completing this goal will be: _____

I will complete this by: My accountability buddy is:

_____   _____

3 things I can do in the next 48 hours: What's stopping me?

1. _____   _____

2. _____   _____

3. _____   _____

Additional small steps I can take to move forward:

_____

_____

_____

AFTER

Date completed: _____ ☐   How did it feel?

                                        _____

                                        _____

What did I learn?

_____   Can I help someone do this?

_____   _____

_____   _____

_____   _____

IN THE END IT'S NOT THE YEARS IN YOUR LIFE THAT COUNT, IT'S THE LIFE IN THE YEARS.

ABRAHAM LINCOLN

LIST ITEM: _____

BEFORE

This is important to me because:

_____

_____

_____

_____

My reward for completing this goal will be: _____

I will complete this by: My accountability buddy is:

_____   _____

3 things I can do in the next 48 hours: What's stopping me?

1. _____   _____

2. _____   _____

3. _____   _____

Additional small steps I can take to move forward:

_____

_____

_____

AFTER

Date completed: _____ ☐   How did it feel?

                                        _____

What did I learn?   _____

_____   _____

_____   Can I help someone do this?

_____   _____

_____   _____

LIST ITEM: _____

BEFORE

This is important to me because:

_____

_____

_____

_____

My reward for completing this goal will be: _____

I will complete this by: My accountability buddy is:

_____   _____

3 things I can do in the next 48 hours: What's stopping me?

1. _____   _____

2. _____   _____

3. _____   _____

Additional small steps I can take to move forward:

_____

_____

_____

AFTER

Date completed: _____ ☐   How did it feel?

                                      _____

What did I learn?   _____

_____

_____   Can I help someone do this?

_____   _____

_____   _____

                                      _____

LIST ITEM: _____

BEFORE

This is important to me because:

_____

_____

_____

_____

My reward for completing this goal will be: _____

I will complete this by: My accountability buddy is:

_____   _____

3 things I can do in the next 48 hours: What's stopping me?

1._____   _____

2._____   _____

3._____   _____

Additional small steps I can take to move forward:

_____

_____

_____

AFTER

Date completed: _____ ☐   How did it feel?

                                       _____

What did I learn?   _____

_____   Can I help someone do this?

_____   _____

_____   _____

_____   _____

LIST ITEM: _____

BEFORE

This is important to me because:

_____

_____

_____

_____

My reward for completing this goal will be: _____

I will complete this by: My accountability buddy is:

_____   _____

3 things I can do in the next 48 hours: What's stopping me?

1. _____   _____

2. _____   _____

3. _____   _____

Additional small steps I can take to move forward:

_____

_____

_____

AFTER

Date completed: _____ ☐   How did it feel?

                                            _____

What did I learn?   _____

_____   Can I help someone do this?

_____   _____

_____   _____

WHETHER YOU THINK YOU CAN OR WHETHER YOU THINK YOU CAN'T, YOU'RE RIGHT.

HENRY FORD

LIST ITEM: _____

BEFORE

This is important to me because:

_____

_____

_____

_____

My reward for completing this goal will be: _____

I will complete this by: My accountability buddy is:

_____   _____

3 things I can do in the next 48 hours: What's stopping me?

1. _____   _____

2. _____   _____

3. _____   _____

Additional small steps I can take to move forward:

_____

_____

_____

AFTER

Date completed: _____ ☐   How did it feel?

                                          _____

                                          _____

What did I learn?   Can I help someone do this?

_____   _____

_____   _____

_____

_____

LIST ITEM: _____

BEFORE

This is important to me because:

_____
_____
_____
_____

My reward for completing this goal will be: _____

I will complete this by:

_____

3 things I can do in the next 48 hours:

1. _____
2. _____
3. _____

My accountability buddy is:

_____

What's stopping me?

_____
_____
_____

Additional small steps I can take to move forward:

_____
_____
_____

AFTER

Date completed: _____ ☐

What did I learn?

_____
_____
_____
_____

How did it feel?

_____
_____
_____

Can I help someone do this?

_____
_____
_____

LIST ITEM: _____

BEFORE

This is important to me because:

_____

_____

_____

_____

My reward for completing this goal will be: _____

I will complete this by: My accountability buddy is:

_____   _____

3 things I can do in the next 48 hours: What's stopping me?

1. _____   _____

2. _____   _____

3. _____   _____

Additional small steps I can take to move forward:

_____

_____

_____

AFTER

Date completed: _____ ☐   How did it feel?

                                                _____

What did I learn?   _____

_____   _____

_____   Can I help someone do this?

_____   _____

_____   _____

LIST ITEM: _____

BEFORE

This is important to me because:

_____

_____

_____

_____

My reward for completing this goal will be: _____

I will complete this by: My accountability buddy is:

_____   _____

3 things I can do in the next 48 hours: What's stopping me?

1. _____   _____

2. _____   _____

3. _____   _____

Additional small steps I can take to move forward:

_____

_____

_____

AFTER

Date completed: _____ ☐   How did it feel?

_____

What did I learn?   _____

_____   _____

_____   Can I help someone do this?

_____   _____

_____   _____

_____   _____

LIST ITEM: _____

BEFORE

This is important to me because:

_____

_____

_____

_____

My reward for completing this goal will be: _____

I will complete this by: My accountability buddy is:

_____   _____

3 things I can do in the next 48 hours: What's stopping me?

1. _____   _____

2. _____   _____

3. _____   _____

Additional small steps I can take to move forward:

_____

_____

_____

AFTER

Date completed: _____ ☐   How did it feel?

                                       _____

What did I learn?   _____

_____

_____   Can I help someone do this?

_____   _____

_____   _____

LIST ITEM: _____

BEFORE

This is important to me because:

_____

_____

_____

_____

My reward for completing this goal will be: _____

I will complete this by: My accountability buddy is:

_____   _____

3 things I can do in the next 48 hours: What's stopping me?

1. _____   _____

2. _____   _____

3. _____   _____

Additional small steps I can take to move forward:

_____

_____

_____

AFTER

Date completed: _____ ☐   How did it feel?

_____

What did I learn?   _____

_____

_____   Can I help someone do this?

_____   _____

_____   _____

USE THE TALENTS YOU POSSESS, FOR THE WOODS WOULD BE VERY SILENT IF NO BIRDS SANG EXCEPT THE BEST.

HENRY VAN DYKE

LIST ITEM: _____

BEFORE

This is important to me because:

_____

_____

_____

_____

My reward for completing this goal will be: _____

I will complete this by: My accountability buddy is:

_____   _____

3 things I can do in the next 48 hours: What's stopping me?

1. _____   _____

2. _____   _____

3. _____   _____

Additional small steps I can take to move forward:

_____

_____

_____

AFTER

Date completed: _____ ☐   How did it feel?

                                          _____

What did I learn?   _____

_____

_____   Can I help someone do this?

_____   _____

_____   _____

LIST ITEM: _____

BEFORE

This is important to me because:

_____

_____

_____

_____

My reward for completing this goal will be: _____

I will complete this by: My accountability buddy is:

_____   _____

3 things I can do in the next 48 hours: What's stopping me?

1. _____   _____

2. _____   _____

3. _____   _____

Additional small steps I can take to move forward:

_____

_____

_____

AFTER

Date completed: _____ ☐   How did it feel?

                                            _____

What did I learn?   _____

_____

_____   Can I help someone do this?

_____   _____

_____   _____

LIST ITEM: _____

BEFORE

This is important to me because:

_____

_____

_____

_____

My reward for completing this goal will be: _____

I will complete this by: My accountability buddy is:

_____   _____

3 things I can do in the next 48 hours: What's stopping me?

1. _____   _____

2. _____   _____

3. _____   _____

Additional small steps I can take to move forward:

_____

_____

_____

AFTER

Date completed: _____ ☐   How did it feel?

                                            _____

What did I learn?   _____

_____

_____   Can I help someone do this?

_____   _____

_____   _____

_____   _____

LIST ITEM: _____

BEFORE

This is important to me because:

_____

_____

_____

_____

My reward for completing this goal will be: _____

I will complete this by: My accountability buddy is:

_____   _____

3 things I can do in the next 48 hours: What's stopping me?

1. _____   _____

2. _____   _____

3. _____   _____

Additional small steps I can take to move forward:

_____

_____

_____

AFTER

Date completed: _____ ☐   How did it feel?

                                            _____

What did I learn?   _____

_____   _____

_____   Can I help someone do this?

_____   _____

_____   _____

LIST ITEM: _____

BEFORE

This is important to me because:

_____

_____

_____

_____

My reward for completing this goal will be: _____

I will complete this by: My accountability buddy is:

_____   _____

3 things I can do in the next 48 hours: What's stopping me?

1. _____   _____

2. _____   _____

3. _____   _____

Additional small steps I can take to move forward:

_____

_____

_____

AFTER

Date completed: _____ ☐   How did it feel?

                                        _____

What did I learn?   _____

_____

_____   Can I help someone do this?

_____   _____

_____

_____   _____

LIST ITEM: _____

BEFORE

This is important to me because:

_____

_____

_____

_____

My reward for completing this goal will be: _____

I will complete this by: My accountability buddy is:

_____   _____

3 things I can do in the next 48 hours: What's stopping me?

1. _____   _____

2. _____   _____

3. _____   _____

Additional small steps I can take to move forward:

_____

_____

_____

AFTER

Date completed: _____ ☐   How did it feel?

                                            _____

What did I learn?   _____

_____   Can I help someone do this?

_____   _____

_____   _____

_____   _____

LIST ITEM: _____

BEFORE

This is important to me because:

_____

_____

_____

_____

My reward for completing this goal will be: _____

I will complete this by: My accountability buddy is:

_____   _____

3 things I can do in the next 48 hours: What's stopping me?

1. _____   _____

2. _____   _____

3. _____   _____

Additional small steps I can take to move forward:

_____

_____

_____

AFTER

Date completed: _____ ☐   How did it feel?

                                    _____

What did I learn?   _____

_____   Can I help someone do this?

_____   _____

_____   _____

LIST ITEM: _____

BEFORE

This is important to me because:

_____
_____
_____
_____

My reward for completing this goal will be: _____

I will complete this by: My accountability buddy is:

_____   _____

3 things I can do in the next 48 hours: What's stopping me?

1._____   _____

2._____   _____

3._____   _____

Additional small steps I can take to move forward:

_____
_____
_____

AFTER

Date completed: _____ ☐   How did it feel?

                                            _____

What did I learn?   _____

_____   _____

_____   Can I help someone do this?

_____   _____

_____   _____

LIST ITEM: _____

BEFORE

This is important to me because:

_____

_____

_____

_____

My reward for completing this goal will be: _____

I will complete this by: My accountability buddy is:

_____   _____

3 things I can do in the next 48 hours: What's stopping me?

1. _____   _____

2. _____   _____

3. _____   _____

Additional small steps I can take to move forward:

_____

_____

_____

AFTER

Date completed: _____ ☐

What did I learn?

_____

_____

_____

_____

How did it feel?

_____

_____

Can I help someone do this?

_____

_____

_____

LIST ITEM: _____

BEFORE

This is important to me because:

_____

_____

_____

_____

My reward for completing this goal will be: _____

I will complete this by: My accountability buddy is:

_____   _____

3 things I can do in the next 48 hours: What's stopping me?

1._____   _____

2._____   _____

3._____   _____

Additional small steps I can take to move forward:

_____

_____

_____

AFTER

Date completed: _____ ☐   How did it feel?

                                            _____

What did I learn?   _____

_____

_____   Can I help someone do this?

_____   _____

_____   _____

A YEAR FROM NOW YOU WILL WISH YOU HAD STARTED TODAY.

KAREN LAMB

LIST ITEM: _____

BEFORE

This is important to me because:

_____

_____

_____

_____

My reward for completing this goal will be: _____

I will complete this by: My accountability buddy is:

_____   _____

3 things I can do in the next 48 hours: What's stopping me?

1. _____   _____

2. _____   _____

3. _____   _____

Additional small steps I can take to move forward:

_____

_____

_____

AFTER

Date completed: _____ ☐   How did it feel?

                                          _____

What did I learn?   _____

_____   Can I help someone do this?

_____   _____

_____   _____

_____   _____

LIST ITEM: _____

BEFORE

This is important to me because:

_____

_____

_____

_____

My reward for completing this goal will be: _____

I will complete this by: My accountability buddy is:

_____   _____

3 things I can do in the next 48 hours: What's stopping me?

1. _____   _____

2. _____   _____

3. _____   _____

Additional small steps I can take to move forward:

_____

_____

_____

AFTER

Date completed: _____ ☐   How did it feel?

                                            _____

What did I learn?   _____

_____   Can I help someone do this?

_____   _____

_____   _____

_____   _____

LIST ITEM: _____

BEFORE

This is important to me because:

_____

_____

_____

_____

My reward for completing this goal will be: _____

I will complete this by: My accountability buddy is:

_____   _____

3 things I can do in the next 48 hours: What's stopping me?

1. _____   _____

2. _____   _____

3. _____   _____

Additional small steps I can take to move forward:

_____

_____

_____

AFTER

Date completed: _____ ☐   How did it feel?

                                                _____

What did I learn?   _____

_____

_____   Can I help someone do this?

_____   _____

_____   _____

NOTHING IN THE WORLD CAN TAKE THE PLACE OF PERSISTENCE. PERSISTENCE AND DETERMINATION ALONE ARE OMNIPOTENT.

CALVIN COOLIDGE

This is space to write down all the extra thoughts running around in your head. Not only will this help clear your mind and relieve built-up stress, but it may also help you move toward your goals.

If you ever feel down, please know that you're not alone.
I still get depressed from time to time. Everyone is fighting a
battle you cannot see. Try talking about it with someone who
cares about you or with a therapist. That's always helped me.

Ben.

IN THE BOOK OF LIFE, THE ANSWERS AREN'T IN THE BACK.

CHARLIE BROWN

YOUR TRUE COURSE

This journal is more than your bucket list. It's about discovering who you are and expressing what you're here to do on Earth. It is about fighting back against those things that pull you away from your true self.

Your goal is to become more and more you. This is a lifelong journey, and you'll have to work hard to protect the time required to pursue your dreams. It might feel selfish at times, but remember, you can't take care of other people if you don't take care of yourself. When you do what you love, you inspire other people to do what they love. You will impact more people than you may ever know.

If you ever feel stuck, picture yourself on your deathbed. Ask your future self, "Will I be content with the time I'm spending on me?" If the answer is no, ask your future self, "What will I be content with?"

That answer is worth fighting for.

Don't ever give up on your list. Your future self will thank you.

Ben.

WAIT.
THERE'S MORE...

Scan this for more support with your goals.
This is just the beginning...

REFERENCES

1) Davidai, S., & Gilovich, T. (2018). "The ideal road not taken: The self-discrepancies involved in people's most enduring regrets." *Emotion*, 18(3), 439–452. https://doi.org/10.1037/emo0000326

2) Ware, Bonnie. (2012) *The Top Five Regrets of the Dying: A Life Transformed by the Dearly Departing*. Hay House, Inc.

3) Phillips, P. P., & American Society for Training and Development. (2010). *ASTD handbook for measuring and evaluating training*. Alexandria, VA: American Society for Training & Development.

ABOUT BEN

Ben Nemtin is a #1 *New York Times* bestselling author, mental health advocate, and one of the world's top motivational speakers. As the co-founder of The Buried Life and a star of MTV's *The Buried Life*, Ben's message of radical possibility has been featured worldwide from *The Today Show* to *The Oprah Winfrey Show*.

As a freshman in university, Ben experienced an unexpected depression that forced him to drop out of school. In an attempt to regain control of his life, Ben created the world's greatest bucket list with his three childhood friends. They borrowed a rickety old RV and criss-crossed North America, chasing their wildest dreams. Every time they accomplished a dream, they helped a complete stranger cross something off their bucket list. From playing basketball with President Obama to having a beer with Prince Harry, from reuniting a father and son after seventeen years to surprising a young girl with a much-needed bionic arm, Ben's mission is to inspire others to live a life of fulfilment.

You can find Ben on social media at @bennemtin or online at www.bennemtin.com. You can find Ben in person in Venice Beach, CA.